Chameleons

Leo Statts

abdopublishing.com

Published by Abdo Zoom™, PO Box 398166, Minneapolis, Minnesota 55439. Copyright © 2017 by Abdo Consulting Group, Inc. International copyrights reserved in all countries. No part of this book may be reproduced in any form without written permission from the publisher. Abdo Zoom™ is a trademark and logo of Abdo Consulting Group, Inc.

Printed in the United States of America, North Mankato, Minnesota
062016
092016

Cover Photo: Shutterstock Images
Interior Photos: Shutterstock Images, 1, 5; Sebastian Duda/Shutterstock Images, 4; Nick Henn/Shutterstock Images, 6, 18–19; Oleg Elena Tovkach/Shutterstock Images, 7; Tom Linster/Shutterstock Images, 8; Jordi Prat Puig/Shutterstock Images, 9; iStockphoto, 10–11; Red Line Editorial, 11, 20 (left), 20 (right), 21 (left), 21 (right); Jana Vodickova/Shutterstock Images, 12; Guille Lopez/Shutterstock Images, 14–15; Luke Wait/Shutterstock Images, 16

Editor: Brienna Rossiter
Series Designer: Madeline Berger
Art Direction: Dorothy Toth

Publisher's Cataloging-in-Publication Data
Names: Statts, Leo, author.
Title: Chameleons / by Leo Statts.
Description: Minneapolis, MN : Abdo Zoom, [2017] | Series: Desert animals | Includes bibliographical references and index.
Identifiers: LCCN 2016941148 | ISBN 9781680791792 (lib. bdg.) | ISBN 9781680793475 (ebook) | ISBN 9781680794366 (Read-to-me ebook)
Subjects: LCSH: Chameleons--Juvenile literature.
Classification: DDC 597.95--dc23
LC record available at http://lccn.loc.gov/2016941148

Table of Contents

Chameleons

Chameleons are **reptiles**.

Some can change their skin color. This helps them hide.

Body

Chameleons can be as small as a penny.

Others are as big as house cats. Most are bright colors.

They have
curled tails.

They wrap their tails around branches. That keeps them safe.

Habitat

Chameleons live in warm places. You can find them in jungles and deserts.

Where chameleons live

Chameleons watch
for food and danger.
Their eyes can look two
different ways at once.

Food

Chameleons
eat berries. They eat
leaves. They also
eat insects.

Their tongues catch live food. The tongues can be as long as their bodies.

Life Cycle

Most chameleons lay eggs. Babies are on their own after they hatch.

They can live
more than ten
years in zoos.

Quick Stats

Average Length – Longest

A Madagascan chameleon is longer than a basketball.

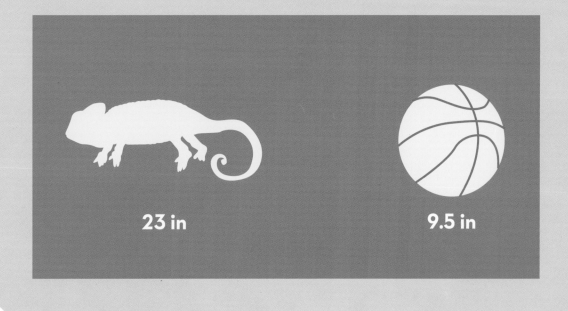

23 in   9.5 in

Average Length – Smallest

A pygmy leaf chameleon is a little longer than a penny.

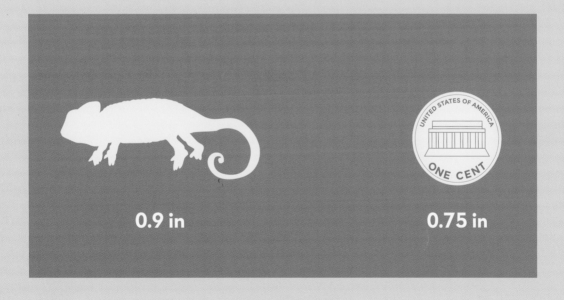

0.9 in

0.75 in

Glossary

desert - a very dry, sandy area with little plant growth.

hatch - to be born from an egg.

jungle - land covered with a lot of trees and other plants.

reptile - a cold-blooded animal with scales. They typically lay eggs.

Booklinks

For more information
on chameleons, please visit
booklinks.abdopublishing.com

Zoom In on Animals!

Learn even more with the Abdo Zoom
Animals database. Check out
abdozoom.com for more information.

Index